until
the roof
lifted off

Poems and Illustrations by
Carly Volpe

Published by

Read often, Read well

Published by Read Furiously. First Edition.

ISBN: 978-0-9965227-7-9

Poetry
Poetry Collection – Single Author

For more information on *Until the roof lifted off* or Read Furiously, please visit readfuriously.com. For inquiries, please contact samantha@readfuriously.com.

Cover design by Carly Volpe
Layout by Adam Wilson

Edited by Samantha Atzeni

Read (v): The act of interpreting and understanding the written word.

Furiously (adv): To engage in an activity with passion and excitement.

**Read Often. Read Well.
Read Furiously**

For Elliott and Margot

For My dad and Chris: one who always answered when
I called and the other who taught me it was ok to use
swimmies when in the deep water.

Table of Contents

Harbor   2

Morning Light, Golden   4

Addiction is Like That   6

Still   7

Span   9

Blankets, Coats, Old Gods   10

Bell–Trained   13

Undone   15

The Boxer   17

I Do Not Read Well On Paper   19

When I Call   21

"It Gets Easier the Deeper You Go"   23

Johnny Jump–Ups   26

Haunting the Bones   28

Taking Inventory   29

It is Springtime and You are Gone   31

29 Oakland Ave   33

Seasons   35

The Mushroom   37

Company Picnic   39

Tight   41

The Fourth Stage   43

Father and Daughter on the Eve of
Heart Surgery   45

Tipping the Rim   47

The Room Where Michael Died   49

The Year of the Firefly   51

Pregnant in July   53

Kept   54

I Could Hang Gilt Mirrors   56

Tarot   59

Hazards of Love   60

What We Allow   61

Pulling Up Bodies   63

We Rarely Think of Death in Spring   65

As a child, I was fat-kneed and restless
tiny braided bedtime parade of loud song
and listening with cupped palm
at my bedroom wall.
Freckled little agent of worry,
nail-bed bitten
and wise to Summer's tricks:
yellow jacket sleight of hand
sour berry on the bush
and second cousin with a bowl cut and
black barrel BB gun.
He plays catch me as you can
ruddy and breathless from wide limb running
slips middle finger and fore
beneath my egg-white training bra strap.

My grandmother told me
"take all your trouble, girl
Give it over to Jesus.
He is as deep and as wide
as the ocean.
All your pain won't be a drop to him."
But I have known oceans
—one moment sure footed;
the next suspended
briny, tumbling, airless.
I've never seen God at the Jersey shore
smiling absently over the counter
behind a sea foam gingham apron
churning out salt water taffy
twisted tightly in their wax paper wrappers.

One day my brother came running home
up the rocky river bank
down the right-of-way, barefoot.

Quiver-eyed field rabbit,
silent little *oh* of a mouth,
dark haze of hornets in his wake.
My small hands in numb tremor,
I plucked the bullheaded terrors
from his summer blonde hair.
Pulled them stinging from his arms.
Pulled them stinging from his back
and left ear and upper lip.
Pulled them crawling, somehow impotent,
from my breast-less chest.

There are days
I don't hear our ragged breath.
Some mornings I don't wake
pulling down bodies from the sky.

When we got off the phone
I took in to beating my leg
into a mess of throbbing blue knots
and cried until
my nightgown was soaked
with drool and tears.
This is what mental illness looks like
at 1:45 am and sleep
will not come down.

Later is morning and I am busy
finding meaning in birds perched on the street lights,
deciphering cloud codes,
crossing boundaries with strangers
in line at the grocery.
I do things out of character
like purchase powerball tickets
and refuse to phone friends.
The frost is still white,
the morning light golden.
My leg burns when I lift it to
walk up the road to the mailbox
and I try to remember the last time I've eaten,
note the hollow space between my hip bones,
wonder when we will speak again
and how I will spend my lottery winnings.

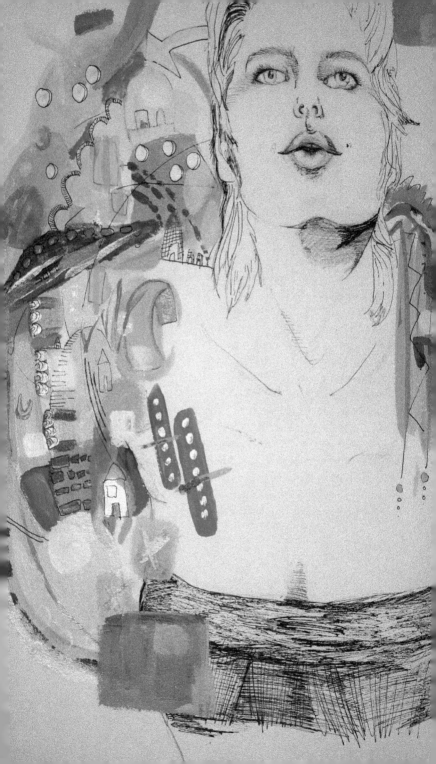

Addiction is like that:
a writhing thing,
quiet clenched teeth or else
prowling oiled pavement in the night,
sniffing at lit windows. You think you've
slammed enough doors,
sealed all exposed beams,
stuffed up the holes,
but still, water pours in.

A girl tucks her urges into a cedar chest
at the foot of the bed
next to curled photos and tenderly mended stockings.
She might not have a beer in seven years
and steer clear of bars and dimly lit parties.
She smiles at strangers now.
Then one night sits two minutes too long
with a bottle of bourbon at a dinner party
and gives over.

What I'm saying is that I think I love you again.

You are the bottle of pills in the bathroom cabinet.
Even though the specter of
glossy-eyed high
and crashing remorse
seem miles far
I keep your count by heart.
I see the darling shiny heft of your shape
and note shadowed imperfections.
I track you in my sleep.

I talk to you, my love,
and whisper promises:
not yet, but maybe soon.

Still

You've never had creamed spinach
until you've eaten it with a plastic spoon
shifted it in a brown prefab slotted tray
brushing elbows with a man who cried his fat-teared way
through group therapy.
He kept repeating: "I'm sorry.
I'm not crazy, just tired."

My attention divided between the still damp pinkness
lingering in his hooked nose
and the flavor of tinny earth and powdered milk
— muscle memory reminds me
of concave shoulders in high school cafeteria.
Feet shuffle by on stained chipped gray tile
almost as though in a dance agreed upon,
unrelenting and steady thrum,
song heard from another room.

On my second morning
a man slouching along the line
dropped like a twine wrapped stone.
His head cracked hard,
sounded off like a hollow melon against slate
heels clacked and slipped in seismic dance.
I grunted and clapped my palms to my ears
but did not look away.
Why didn't my mom offer creamed spinach
as an option as dinner accompaniment?
Warm and soft, innocuous and safe.

And why did this man insist, before each circle session
"I'm not crazy, just tired?"
As though he were the only one with bags beneath his eyes
chattering hip bones and chewed away lips
or invisible splinters beneath his thumbnails
that required pinch and rub to relieve?

You might not be crazy,
but you are the only one still crying.

Span

I am a pretty, useless thing.
Chrome mid-century toaster with a frayed cloth cord.
Crepe paper crown.
Glass ball.
Origami bird.

Small purple enamel pill case with a broken brass hinge.
The apology delivered to an empty room
after you've closed the door.

Large burgundy velvet button.
Half intention.
Leaky porcelain cup.

Single lace glove.
Hand thrown clay pot, unsealed.
Sodden lunar moth crawling
circling the porch screen,
stretching wings to the bootless moon.

Wearing two bothered cardigans
and a master chair haircut grown wild,
her arms always hugged tightly to meager sides
warding off the chill of a temperate room.

My roommate was an uncommon mountain
in the one wired window's glow.
Her wrinkled wit and clean serene face
had earned her extra blankets.

We spoke in the hush-world of "lights out"
amidst the Thorazine shufflers
and croons of bedsprings and muffled weeping.
I learned lines in the ceiling, saw the shadows cast there
witnessed the crows appear and become something more like
waves
as she spoke of her family's fickle inattentions.
Top Irish Catholic lawyer once
they seemed only to find concern when
she donned many coats
found an old god
observed the Sabbath
worried over missing furniture
that disappeared in the night.

The waves became blankets, coats, old gods,
small bells ringing.

And she tells me God has brought me here
to this shared stale hospital room
so she could lay her small, dry palm on

the stitched slices in my forearm,
to speak through earnest straight teeth
and my foggy brain
as the two pills in the Dixie cup
the night nurse handed me
begin to settle in and give loose sway to the surface of things.

I feel the static of universes where she touches me
anoints me with the knowledge that everything will be ok
if I hold tightly to the bitter crust of the earth.
My crumpled prophet tells me I am holy
we are all, from lips to toes, perfection
and asks if she could have
just one of my blankets.

Bell-Trained

I have gears below my skin
clear wheels that spin,
hitch, move without benefit of program or planning.
Mechanical mistress, stringless,
I pop and lock gracefully
face down in my bed
run my legs as though an animal dreaming of escape,
or perhaps pursuit.

At the mercy of the wiry weather inside my chest
storm of fireflies and mechanized beeps
— and god, the deep fat droning in my belly,
I wait against odds.
Like a dog, bell-trained,
I leap at the sound of a message *ding*
dry mouthed and hungry for a gentle word;
I know it will not be you.

Man who is nothing now
but the motley assortment of things you left behind.
You are a single photo in my phone,
a black leather belt,
and the creased mall receipt
I keep in my purse.
You are the memory of boots sounding off hollow on stairs
and the hundred sweaty emails I cannot erase.

You loved me once,
my wheels know,
but not advisedly or well.
Not well enough.

Undone

The carrot flowers grew in, so fat and frothy
this summer,
they armed out sideways
competing for the sun.
I stared at them, your empty seat quietly
passing time and judgment,
thinking "shit finds a way."
That's what shit does;
it finds a way through concrete
and beer bottle wrappers and broken teeth.

Hands will seek out old scars,
that's what hands do:
learn raised contours,
attempt to smooth the puckered edges and
flatten them in measureless prayer.

Someday there will be a place to put this grief.
For now, I tuck the blade of my palm
between my thighs,
hide your love letters between dog-eared book pages,
and hold entire conversations with your shadow
in the grocery store
hissing out choppy monologues below my breath
while regarding cereal boxes and canned fruit.

We are undone;
potted ferns on our sills,
roots with no place left to go but
tangled around in their tight pale mandalas.
Which fickle planet, in her course,
placed you in my broken path?
And under which same hazy moon
have you been peeled away?

The Boxer

The boxer has a way with words
writes poetry about his Greek uncle
and the longing he felt
as a boy
to be consumed by the father who didn't want him.
He had lied on his dating profile,
said he was raised by two mothers
implying a softness he doesn't possess.

Speaking on his breath and keeping his elbows up,
he drinks whiskey neat
and begins to tell stories of a childhood
in his grandfather's care, the old man himself a failed fighter.
His nose crooks and
points to a brutal learning time.
He tells me of the amateur fight in which
with a punch landed off its mark
he broke another youth's skull in ways
from which neither will likely heal.

When we lie naked together,
the boxer is a song composed of hard notes
and lightweight tones.
He touches my body earnestly
and meets the shadows in my eyes without retreat.
I stretch starfished fingers across
my belly,
trying to hide the soft sway and fullness there.
He traces the curve of flesh with his teeth
tests the build and give of it
says "I love this part of you most of all."

I am surprised when
instead of meeting me for the show
I come to be alone, sitting in a darkened art center
beside an empty folding chair
eyes scanning the crowd.
He ducks
my calls the next day
and every call following
until I realize my arms are too short
for this fight.

I Do Not Read Well On Paper

Lines deeply grooved between brows
from repetitive bouts of anger and wincing;
owed to skin aging and nerves worn through.

Single mom of two loud, tangled children.
One failed marriage to a sullen musician
tucked firmly under my belt.
Former smoker whose nose secretly seeks out the scent,
never let loose the craving for flame and ash.

Bruised cumulus clouds often cover creativity
and can swallow entire weeks whole.

The skin on my breasts and thighs, when pinched,
no longer returns, but tents,
shifts and settles softly.
My breath is not sweet, words guarded
when naked and trying not to
meet the gaze of a new lover.

My hands slotted spoons,
spilling more
than they hold these days.

My father and I have an unspoken deal:
when I call, he answers.
Perhaps a pipe has burst into the basement
cloudy water raining ceaselessly from the ceiling
and two children, roundheaded and quick
beat their feet in the new muck.
Buckets filling up fast,
guide my hand to the small sure lever that stops the tide.

The car is slurring and lurching again:
not quite whirring
not quite whining
but a click and a moan and a tick like a bomb—
predict the future.
Can we limp our way to payday?
Or must coin jars now be shattered;
seat cushions tossed for lost currency?
Our offerings then left for the god of Machines,
of soldered wheels and iron rods,
with wishes for future lucky lubrication
—though he is a vengeful god.

My father trusts I will text
with news of some small success,
photos of calf-eyed granddaughter,
or word of birds in the field that need naming.
He understands I only call when things are broken
and require mending
beyond what my two feeble hands can fix.
My mistakes have a way of snaking,
climbing attic stairs and descending

weaving through, shedding moist skin
in afternoon's calm corners.

When shadows start edging out
the places light pours in,
he catches my heart in cracked calloused palms,
holds halves together when I fear I cannot do it alone.

To look at a horse
its swimming any length
seems improbable.
More designed of speed and hammer,
thistle, and deep creased earth.

But Neptune is also the god of horses.

My son licks his salty lips,
throws sand at the ocean;
he is coltish and shifting
in the steadily slipping grit.
Still he slaps at his narrow chest
howls into the wind,
fierce in the face of infinity
the way only gap-toothed youth allows.

My father helps him to navigate the tide
edges him two steps out beyond comfort
"Are you a man or a mouse,"
he sing-songs gruffly
"You have to dive under the water before
it crashes down on you."

Father had dressed impractically for the beach
tightly laced white trainers
and distressed leather belt
fighting to hold up linen shorts
lately given to sag.
He leaves his shoes with me
allows the water to break against his calves

cups the undersides of creased knees
as grandson frolics and gulls harass shore.

I sit in the sand and squint out
below my cupped palm
having lost sight of my father
—his sudden withdrawal
from boy, foam, and broken shell
like an abrupt shift in an important conversation
I wasn't aware we were having.

Beyond pointed crest and rhythmic swell,
sun neatly skitters her way over green water
and crowns his tawny hair.
He swims so deep
I fear he might swim out forever;
past the ships on the horizon.
Past the horizon.

But he reappears
and there is some thready relief
though vague fear nests and roils.
Cancer has
stolen teeth and leaned his frame
taken some strength from arm
and whittled away breadth of shoulder.

In this moment I could think him
a stranger,
a rawboned boy spending summers with his mother
on the shores of Puerto Rico,
or an improbable animal,
minor salty god of deep green and breath,

swelling with each wave.
If I squinted my eyes,
cocked my head and saw him that way,
new unexpected current,
I'd find him
easily rolling back to me.

Johnny Jump-Ups

I told you once
in the hangover of my grandfather's dying,
losing him
meant one less person
knew my name
held me in their heart's dark room,
counted me among their few blessings
on this small dirty earth.

And now we are rotating
a globe green with new wood.
Geese still pick up the lake and fly off with it every fall
but his shoes are stretched wide-mouthed and empty;
their uneven fat laces
open palmed questions
with no answers or telling.

He spent months peering through the slats
of cheap beige plastic blinds.
The neighbors' chickens were in the road again,
again let loose to crossover
to scratch in his patch of green
which he still tended weekly
atop ancient red mower
—oxygen tank riding shotgun.

In my dreams, he is walking booted
through Johnny jump-ups and early spring trees.
He tells me with a mouth that is made
of wheat shafts and honey
that he loves me.

He didn't say it except maybe later
in the humid jungle of my dreams.
But still, riding in the small nook
curled child, warm comma,
behind the bench seat of his El Camino
sleepy smiles tattooed to my knees,
I knew.

As I sang the southern spiritual that
chanted down his life's last saw-toothed breath,
I didn't believe in god.
My only truth and gospel
was written in an afternoon's golden light,
fixed now in the hard amber of my youth
−the story of how we reclined on the living room shag.

Flocked couch cushions under our bellies,
supper plates lowered shockingly to the floor,
he smiled at me.
He said we would eat
like the Romans did.

Haunting the Bones

To the new inhabitants in
the home of my youth:

Do not be afraid if,
in your shifting periphery
while perched upon your
tacky, chipped kitchen stool,
I am there
bathing in the deep
porcelain sink.

Please disregard the melodrama
of my tumbling upend over and down the stairs
in haste to answer the ringing phone.
Ignore the sticky sweet hint
in the air
of singed apple pie attempts.

I am a shadow in your house
a lingering reminder
that a large life was lived
here.
I am haunting the bones of my
youth.
I will not abide
forgetting.

My boss at the gas station told me
not to smile so much.
"It gives men the wrong idea."
At night I counted out packs of cigarettes
backlit silhouette in the gas station's
big bay window.
Cars and trucks came and went and
I would lose track of the number of
the packs in my hands.
I kept notoriously terrible count
taking hashmark tally with a tiny pencil
only to start again
when the columns tilted all wrong.
At night that window could be a mirror.

At night that window could be a lake
I was swimming its brackish depths
without air or hope of air.
I mopped the floor but
could not touch the water;
was warned that oil from the tanks
buried deep beneath our feet
had leached into the groundwater
and it just was safer
not to touch it.

His penis lay timidly waiting on my gaze,
nude man in VW van
a casual interloper
in my humbling nighttime routine.
Me and that patient little pencil.

On his rigid thigh
there was a faded tattoo
of what could have been a rose.
Hasty clothes piled next to him,
moments stretched and split between us like
spilled oil runs and spreads ever out
and doesn't seem to stop.
I thought of the houses surrounding
the tiny six pump station
and wondered if they too
knew they shouldn't
touch the water.
I was worried the man in the van
might never leave
the glass would fall away
that the tally with each black hash
would never break even again.

The trees are late in blooming this year,
thin reeds of branches still embarrassingly bare
in the town where I was born.
We would share jasmine tea, if you were here,
and discuss the politics of koi in the pond
as flashes of fleshy marigold and mottled pearl
circle and breach the surface
in wide-lipped search of biscuit crumbs.

Maybe, if the day allows, a walk through the woods
behind my childhood home.
Never so deep though,
never losing sight of the old barn between the bare limbs
—its chipping paint the peeling reminder
of how the things we leave unattended decay.

Deep from the thorny vine and bramble
we could hear a lean beast of fur and teeth
crunching through unfortunate bones.
We might walk back along the red stony banks
an arterial creek feeding the Delaware
and I would remember a fat garter snake
my brothers crushed beneath a rock
there in that spot.
The force split her skin, causing a small wet birth
of what seemed a biblical plague.
Horrified, we never spoke of what we saw,
writhing ball, each smaller than a mulberry
and so very much darker.

If you were here, I would cover your eyes with my two hands,
and speak plainly about the terror and loneliness of childhood
—the ringing ears and empty mouth of it.
I would show you the crumbling stone perch
beneath the walking bridge where I hid
and teach you the small songs you must sing
to keep you safe there.

Do not mind the chilly April waters.
Take off your shoes.
We are on holy ground.

The thing I remember
from the inside of your house
is your father throwing you down the stairs
after he caught you kissing another boy
one Thursday after school.

I drive by 29 Oakland Ave every day
on my way home from work.
Those splayed spindles make for poor porch railings.
They always did.
The witchy front flowerbed seems
to have suffered for lack of care.
Shades of the splintered rattan chairs,
two boys lighting cigarettes tip to tip,
half gallon jug of too sweet iced tea,
are all cast permanently
as though etched in thermal shadow.

In my mind your house has a roof,
and sometimes it has walls,
but always stairs,
always falling.

Somewhere in your house there was a mirror
large enough so we both could stand
in its reflection.
You, an impermanent prince,
sweet heavy lid of eye,
the still blade of your jaw bone could cut
and could birth blue shadow from light.
We crushed up chalk pastels

with a razor and the flat bottom of a gin glass
mixed them with our spit
painted my newborn face
so much clean space for magenta and gold.

Somewhere in your house
we napped after all that creation.
But all I can remember
is your ankle catching in the banister.
Your father's fist opening.
Your father's fist closing.

Seasons

She is a woman who comes in seasons;
bitter cold blasts
blowing through glass hearts
like slick brown beer bottles
through a chilly December kitchen window.

The spring of her course
nurses small rabbits freshly born,
pink eyes still closed to the reality
that though they are new
my father and I will bury
them in damp fragrant earth
three days later.
For all her effort, she could not keep
them alive.

My mother, in summer, is unparalleled.
A diet of robin's eggs
and six pomegranate seeds.
Painfully petite
she discharges and explodes.
She illuminates the sky with fireworks
and the ones that melt into twinkling cinders
have always been my favorite;
they leave you with something
after the shimmer is gone.

Her fall is marked
with playful kisses,
pleas of forgiveness,
and a spinning
which keeps us all
off balance
for years.

The Mushroom

My brother sleeps on a musty cot
threadbare mattress the color of ragweed and rot.
He scrabbles by on dim bulb hope
under low slung ceilings
and grey meager portions of dignity
served on impermanent cardboard trays.
In a subterranean room reserved for indigents
and the criminally disaffected,
he is the mushroom.
He is fleshy fruit of hidden dark and fecund ache
hair white, fine, thread–like
rooting him to his sodden pillow
beneath the ground floor
of the Norristown State hospital.

His attic bedroom in our childhood home smelled like spent
vodka,
Marlboro reds stubbed out in dull torpor,
and the resentment that simmered a slip below the skin.
He kept wirebound notebooks with bloodshot scrawl
hidden in a yellow wicker cabinet beside his unmade bed.
I would sneak quiet as winter sunsets,
trace his letters with careful fingertips,
try to glean some secret piece of him
to tuck deep into myself.

My brother had hair that was red
the only sibling in fact
not gold spun or dun of the earth.
He did not resemble flame
or engine.

Not the bright wet skin of a summer berry.
My brother was the fox in the briar,
the brooding ocean under an eastern sunrise,
an untended fall acre, field gone fallow.

Company Picnic

We are river rats;
white gleaming wet bodies slipping wet off rocks,
cutting the soles of our feet on errant glass shards.

We are river rats;
wading through oil rainbows
that cling to stained sodden white undershirts

these boys and me,
thighs slick with pollution
nine years old.

We awkwardly pose and posture,
brought together once a year
behind the printing factory

that stains my father's fingertips and ego.
And when he smiles, he hides the side of his mouth
not wide; tooth missing now.

We watch as tents are hoisted for the union picnic,
they roll in kegs and burn fat hot dogs
to be tucked into soggy buns.

When the sun hits just so
between the dark blue tips of trees,
and when our parents smell like honeysuckle sweat

my mom's lips taste white wine sweet
and her gingham dress strap drops to three o'clock
on her sunburned shoulder.

We self-consciously float toward other kids
other small bodies to ritualistically dare
to sneak off and worship muddy river gods

splash near drainage pipes and catch crayfish
silhouetted by sterile plant towers
and our loud rat laughter.

Tight

"Would you look at her?"
Swedish grandmother in oversized straw bonnet said
of woman in black spandex on the Florida sand.
"Would you look at her legs?"
And I did.
Shadows, circles, ripples,
the uneven pounds of flesh.
She moves along the shoreline toeing shells
weaves through waves
bearing the weight of our gaze.

"I'm fat too," I say, once,
fingering prickling rash between rubbed raw thighs.
I eye the bulge above the band of purple plastic jelly shoe,
and higher, see the true betrayal:
sucked wet indent of navel in suit.
"Yes, but you're tight."
Her knobby knuckles wave the air dismissively
in her vague, sure reply
gold rings caught in summer sun.

We look again to the surf
"God bless her heart"
she says and touches gently the cutting outward curve
of her left collarbone.

In my overstuffed secondhand bed at night
these splayed child fingers became edged
—the shine of my blades flash
as I pinched firmly

learn to cut away enough of myself
to feel whole.

These holes left gaping
fill up tight to bursting when they hear
"she is withering down to nothing."
or "tell me your secret"
as though this
is the most important story of loss
I have to share.

The Fourth Stage

When your father has cancer
I will say *I am sorry* & mean it
but not imagine the clusters of cells
dividing uninvited and disproportionately.
The thick clumps of pink tissue
with their sea creature probing tips
will not invade my routine morning coffee.

I will not hear the anger in his voice
the sharp dip and then cut when he ends with
"Well it isn't good."
As though he peered through the phone
and saw my pearly hope,
heard the pause of breath where he could
interject a joke, or else
a hint of perhaps.
Your father would lie to me.

It would not fall to me
to call your baby brother and interrupt
a morning work meeting.
He admits he let a woman
read his palm in San Diego, last Saturday.
She studied the wild topography of his future
said a member of his family was gravely ill.
Of course, she was talking about your father,
or else her own.

If your father had cancer
I would bake him a Black Forest cake
because I know how he loves chocolate.
Then ice it with buttercream I would hand beat
even if my mixer weren't broken.

I would fold in inky flecks of Madagascar vanilla
scraped from the whole split bean.
Place the maraschinos with medical precision.
I would lick the spoons and wash the bowls
and then put it all away.

Father and Daughter on the Eve of Heart Surgery

Watching the monitors blink
and taking note of your heavy lids,
the thick folds magnified by large spectacles,
held in place by long, untamable brow hairs,
I sit with you in emergency.

We talk about my crumbling marriage and
your eyes moisten when you say
"It must have been hard
to live so long without
Love." I cross and uncross my legs
fold and refold into myself.
"It all seems unfair,"
I say, suddenly protective of my pain.

The monitors ping and lines dart
and I don't need to look in your eyes
to see your heart.
It is loud in protestation and
struggling against rhythm.

We share no more words,
your lips pressed gently
but firmly shut.

Until I mention signs of impending Spring
and seeing fox in the field by your house.
We discuss fashion and politics
through the chirping, bells and beeps.
I can see the blue of your eyes snap as they

widen for dramatic effect.
Rhythm is built in the language to help us remember things.
There are bones in our stories
sinew contained within our narrative.

You make a joke about putting in an order for a bionic heart
as you peruse the battered hospital lunch menu.
I think
you couldn't be any stronger
or more fragile.

When you have a Bully,
you only have to hit him once
my father said to my brothers and me.
But make sure you do it right.
If you do it right,
you only have to hit him once
and you will never have to do it again.

He would then show us rib jabs
and sharp rises of knees
and the brutality of an elbow
and a place on the throat that could collapse
the windpipe,
so don't hit just there.
Go for the belly,
the soft flesh,
so that the very breath will leave him
and he will understand.
He will know and you will know
and you should make sure other kids see
because then they will know too.

I only hit my mother once.
My nose was dripping red and
with a clench of her hair in my hand,
I felt the thick satisfaction
of her cheekbone meeting the white wood
of the door frame.

That day was a tipping along
the rim of our bowl.
What was spilled was
washed away with ugly words
but never
with her fists upon me
again.

The Room Where Michael Died

Whenever we went to the town hospital as children,
and as a child, I went to the town hospital often
(twice over for assumed appendix rupture,
cornea scratched by the bully at the bus stop,
twisted ankle, clenched colon,
and many mysterious pains never solved)
my bearings were found while perched atop mint sheets
wrapped and tied with awkward bows
into wash-worn gowns.

My parents had one story to tell.

"That was the room where your brother died"
my father would point and say intimately,
each instance as though the first,
eyes wet with unpassed time.
It seemed, wherever we were,
there it was.

Occasionally some flat-faced orderly
wheeled our sorry party into the very space.
"This is the room where
they blew air into his lungs
for the third and final time."

I've heard it said *God breaks the heart*
again and again and again
until it stays open.
"He was just a little boy"
the story told
again and again and

again.
"His throat closed,
he had no breath,
no hope for resuscitation"
—the last a word I struggled and circled
and could not pounce on
or re-pronounce with confidence.

The shades and ghosts of that night move fluid here
shadow-play visible on the thin skin
around my mother's mouth.
I breathed in the stories
my parents would tell,
tumbling through quiet time,
their broken verses of longing
winging us up and threatening to let go
drop us tumbling from claw and beak
before returning to the
concrete bleeps and sweet antiseptic.

That was back when the rooms had doors,
no flimsy taupe curtains on their chatty metal runners.
Mother would again tell the room-story
seated in the visitor's chair:
The night Michael died
everyone must've wept until the roof lifted off the building
and now the rooms have no doors.

The Year of the Firefly

It is a good year for fireflies
and that means
a good year to dream
heady dreams and wake up
next to big ideas.

It means it is a year
for children
sticky with chocolate
and the day's adventures
to climb over and under the boundaries
of their own imagination.

On this July by way of June evening,
the day lilies in repose
nod their orange heads in silent sway.
Night is doused with the scent
of earth cooling
and soundly sleeping bumblebees
steeped in honeysuckle.

It is a good year for fireflies,
and the kingdom of light
out in the high grass,
with its staccato bursts and ebbs,
washes over like a song
you knew a long time ago
but now can remember
only half the words.
It makes you remember
sitting in your father's lap

grass tickling bare legs,
eating strawberry preserves with a broad spoon
watching the twilight
bloom and spread.

But then, this is a year
for half remembered songs
and dreams that bear fruit.
This is the year of the firefly
and the time
that makes you ache
for a chance
to begin again.

Pregnant in July

We sat
stroking our bulbous
distended bellies
and compared pains
with graceful turns of
swollen ankle
and grotesque descriptions
of our bodies' small betrayals.

As though debutantes
of some absurd summer picnic,
we fanned ourselves with
sections of old newspaper
and sipped at
tall glasses of lemonade,
wishing for vodka or gin.

Now in parodies of our former bodies,
we need to be propelled forward
to be pried out of seats
and rolled out of beds.
Sweat glistens behind
dimpled knees
and beads along upper lip.

We wait petulantly
for the fruit
of our labor's end.

Kept

A praying mantis sits
staring at me from her constant perch:
dust—thick window ledge
above my kitchen sink.
I placed her there,
the delicate sap of her legs
still pliant and green,
two weeks ago
having fished her, dead
from the well of the window.

Her belly was fat and soft;
I worried that the house ants,
who have built Byzantine nests in my walls,
might seek her out
to swarm in moving blankets of tiny bodies
and carry her off, bit by bit
—her final funerary procession.
Last spring I saw them overwhelm and devour
a clenched inky wolf spider behind the garbage can.

But they don't come.

Her wings have gone golden now.
First at the curved edge and then inward
as though bleached by the sun
or else becoming something new in death, slowly.
She is my companion while I swirl the rag
and twist the sponge to
tidy breakfast dishes or soak a pan to scour
or stare unmoving out

at my children in their frenetic backyard play.
I catch a glimpse of the neighbors' bovine cat,
plump furry paunch swaying low in the grass.

I had watched her too for days
trapped between the wavy glass
and the mesh screen she had climbed
to the very top,
unsure what insect fate had placed her
in this impossible way,

immune to her pain
only thinking of the toys spilling
haphazardly into the hall,
the paperwork building in tedious sloped piles,
and the feeling that my soul
has somehow run off ahead
and I might never catch up.
I was resentful that she asked this of me
her green ball eyes cast about
the prison she had crawled into.
I couldn't save us both.

Eventually I did crack the window,
I did, taking pity
punching the corners
to release the wood's swollen grip.
Slid the screen
up two inches,
escape now possible
if she would only climb down.

I Could Hang Gilt Mirrors

There lives in me
the tendency to move
into people the way I do houses.
Unmindful of sags in kitchen linoleum
poor judge of leaks in the ceiling
or creaks in the floorboards.
Can't you see?
The fireplace is deep and wide,
the space well lit,
needing only minor adjustments:
my grandmother's oriental rug,
a bookshelf, new green love.
Can't you see me
crossed-kneed and knitting?
I don't knit yet, but in this room, I could learn.

I find charm in brassy ornate affectations,
kitschy light fixtures fickle in their working order,
and the wheat-pennies pushed deep
in every door lock.
Time and again I convince myself
the smell will come out.
But that stink is fixed thick in the carpet pile,
ground under scarred boot heel.
Years of hard living have crystallized,
and scrubbing until pink fingertips split
won't help. It is difficult to feel safe
when the guts have been ripped from the bellies
of the smoke detectors, but
I could hang gilt mirrors
over the fist-size gouges in the drywall.

In this home with its ancient wiring
and drafty windows painted closed
I will do better.
Here my heart can hold all this potential
without spilling
or rending.

It takes months to realize
the thin crack in the wallpaper
runs clear through to the foundation.
Daily, the shelves fight symmetry.
Sparrows begin to nest in the attic
and we stop giving common objects new names.
I pull on a well-worn sweater, sip coffee
as I watch the woods from the attic with the birds;
envy them their tidy nests,
their flight and flying.

Tarot

Two years gone now
since you hung in midair
sullen moon tethered to a barn loft
with a found rope.
Two years and I still
wander this moldy house at night
arched bony spine bent, listening at walls,
rummaging the ashes in the hearth,
chewing through electrical cords with the mice
and your ghost
who will not be chased out.

I do not drink wine anymore
but if I did
it would be cheap, and deep
and from many cups,
fingertips stained mulberry
shuttling these morbid cards from one hand
to the other
cutting back again without purpose or end.

The tarot deck did not see you
fall without firm footing
will not catch my descent or predict perhaps
some still unseen rising;
me, ugly little rooster egg,
plumb growing lowest to the earth,
made new
in some rare alchemy.

The Hazards of Love

In my rear view
everything grades faintly
into tiny inorganic hives and trees
hieroglyphic and listing and then gone.
As the car sucks down 95
spitting out exhaust
in a winter cold-sweat.

I am the trembling homemade slingshot.
I am the churlishly spinning pebble.
I am hurtling toward you.

The quiet lens of your living room is clean,
lean lines sparse;
a gut under filled.
I want to tear off my socks and toss them,
climb to grip the sofa cushion with pink pebble toes,
curl my lips and paint them red,
perform binding spells with items
all pilfered from your kitchen spice rack.
I could take fat shears to my hair,
curl into you, weeping comma, in your black leather chair
or rend my blouse and bare my breasts
to the night-mirror of a window.
You are the foot.
I am the shoe.

I am the surging and the dwindling,
both the woman
and the wasp at Summer's end.

What We Allow

I

My first boyfriend was in love
with Sylvia Plath
–poised, serpentine, precocious and death obsessed.
Having no real grasp of the gas range,
born unwittingly into coil and covalent,
I once inserted my head into the gaping maw of my mother's
oven.
The cool tarnished rack pleated my fleshy cheek.
I couldn't understand how Sylvie saw the deed done,
at once embarrassed,
covetous of her resolve to withstand the heat.

II

His mouth drooped slightly to the left
spit pooling and threatening spill.
Eyes rolled and scanned
scrolled and panned our faces
to glean cues for his thick–lipped response.
His hands groped the careless air for balance
as he dragged one black double knotted Nike
slightly behind the next
his gait uncomfortable to watch.
My father's college friend, weight of mortgage woes
and in the throes of a romantic crisis
left unexplained to me, thirteen,
had pulled his Chevy into the garage
and waited for an end to trouble.
Instead he now wished loudly for death
and barked "Jesus"

cracked pussy jokes
his anoxic brain forgetting its context
at the third largest IHOP in all of Bucks County.

III

Some evenings in winter
I drive along the river's road,
the sluggish gray mantle lurching along
battered reed and boreal stone bank.
It overwhelms, the thought
of wading into frozen water
the bite and the numb of it
to the chin and then only hair
licked out along the rushing surface.
And then gone.
It seems possible.

IV

I have outlived Plath
and Jesus too
in sheer years.
And while no one will remember my name,
no teenage boys moon over grainy photos of me,
I will have curled page ends
and canker sores to mark them.
I will have grit of sand under tender foot
and bite of lime tucked in cheek.
I will have as many
sunsets stretching forward as are allowed.

Pulling Up Bodies

Curling myself around the shift in your eyes,
I tell you all about
the things that still manage to scare me:

The soft focus terror of trap doors
in barn loft floors seen from below.
A dire newspaper horoscope read aloud
two days too late to save us.
Small coffins lowered into unrelenting earth.
The torn edges where shame and anxiety tenderly knit.
Bad checks written in listing hotel rooms
by tan men and their gold pinky ring smiles.
My draped crepe paper skin and tight jaw,
these molars now worn down to sullen cups,

and I would sell this salty soul for new teeth
to chew away my crooked lips.
Start fresh and raw but free
from pell—mell rambling
and graceless overabundance
of verb and voice.

God grant me the serenity
of scissors for fingers
clipping away the inessential
things I tried on and kept;
my father's long pregnant pauses
my mother's insecure breathiness of sibilant s's
slip off this ragweed daisy chain coronet
collection of regret and rage.

We are one moving, uneven beast
under my wash-worn quilt.
Reciting stories unearthed from old beds,
pulling bodies from frozen rivers,
setting them upright,
believing they will run away with us.
Half mad,
half sure,
we too will come alive in the morning.

We Rarely Think of Death in Spring

Fingers starfish into the grit—
meet knotty tuber,
pluck fat pearl of curled grub,
and predict the future:
beetles blossom in spring to
render teacup—roses skeletal husks.
I don't begrudge them their destructive hunger.
But neither do I tuck them back unmolested,
rather set each out to the mercy of beady eyed black birds.

Once committed to my task
kneeling in the garden as if a supplicant
to the day lilies and the creeping thyme
I am determined.
Gently I coil dandelion stalk
and stubborn onion grass
around my middle finger and pinch,
rip up then, savagely from the root
to dissuade their splayed rebirth.

Surrounded by scores of anemic mourning dresses
seated in my bed of pernicious widow's weeds,
I swipe the sting of sweat from my eyes,
return again to bend and divide the earth
under the careful watch of
sunflowers cowed in deep bow
and so many patient crows.

Carly Volpe

Carly Volpe has been writing since she was a child. Her first published pieces can be found in her junior high literary magazines and punk zines published by other kids. She continued to write and has studied and workshopped in her local vibrant community of artists and poets. Volpe is the winner of the Stan Heim Poetry Award and has received recognition in other competitions such as the Bucks County Poet Laureate and Main Street Poets. A Bucks County native, where she currently lives with her two children, Volpe is in love with walking outside at night and picking wild berries.

A Note to Our Furious Readers

From all of us at Read Furiously, we hope you enjoyed our latest poetry collection, *Until the roof lifted off.*

There are countless narratives in this world and we would like to share as many of them as possible with our Furious Readers.

It is with this in mind that we pledge to donate a portion of these book sales to causes that are special to Read Furiously and the creators involved in *Until the roof lifted off.* These causes are chosen with the intent to better the lives of others who are struggling to tell their own stories.

Reading is more than a passive activity – it is the opportunity to play an active role within our world. At Read Furiously, its editors and its creators wish to add an active voice to the world we all share because we believe any growth within the company is aimless if we can't also nurture positive change in our local and global communities. The causes we support are not politically driven, but are culturally and socially–based to encourage a sense of civic responsibility associated with the act of reading. Each cause has been researched thoroughly, discussed openly, and voted upon carefully by our team of Read Furiously editors.

To find out more about who, what, why, and where Read Furiously lends its support, please visit our website at readfuriously.com/charity

Happy reading and giving, Furious Readers!

Read Often, Read Well, Read Furiously!

CPSIA information can be obtained
at www.ICGtesting.com
Printed in the USA
FFHW010646291218
49997577-54711FF